Ladybird  Readers

Baby Animals

Series Editor: Sorrel Pitts
Written by Hazel Geatches

LADYBIRD BOOKS

UK | USA | Canada | Ireland | Australia
India | New Zealand | South Africa

Ladybird Books is part of the Penguin Random House group of companies
whose addresses can be found at global.penguinrandomhouse.com.
www.penguin.co.uk   www.puffin.co.uk   www.ladybird.co.uk

Penguin
Random House
UK

First published by Ladybird Books, 2017
001

Text copyright © Ladybird Books Ltd, 2017

Printed in China

A CIP catalogue record for this book is available from the British Library

ISBN: 978-0-241-29745-2

All correspondence to:
Ladybird Books
Penguin Random House Children's
80 Strand, London WC2R 0RL

MIX
Paper from
responsible sources
FSC® C018179
FSC
www.fsc.org

Ladybird Readers

BBC earth

Baby Animals

Inspired by BBC Earth TV series and
developed with input from BBC Earth
natural history specialists

Contents

Picture words

lion

lion cub

elephant

elephant calves

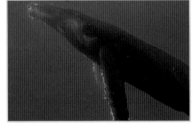

whale

whale calf

monkey   **group** of monkeys

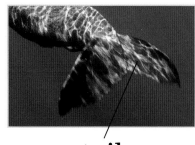

fur   tail

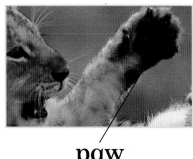
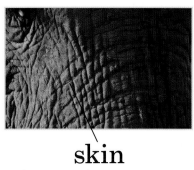

paw   skin

trunk   tusk

Baby animals

Some baby animals are small.
Some baby animals are big.

monkeys

elephants

Can you see the baby animals?

lions

whales

Monkeys

Baby monkeys
are small.

This baby monkey
has got brown fur
and a pink face.

fur

Monkey families

A baby monkey lives with its mother.

They live in a big family
group with many monkeys.

Lions

Lion cubs are small.

fur

They have got brown
fur and big paws.

paw

Lion families

A lion cub lives in a big family group with many lions.

cub

The mother is with her cubs.

lion

Elephants

Elephant calves are big.

An elephant calf has got gray skin and a small trunk. It has not got tusks.

calf

This elephant calf is with its mother.

elephant

Elephant families

An elephant calf lives with its mother.

They live in a big family group with many elephants.

These elephant calves are sleeping
and their mothers are near.

21

Whales

Whale calves are very big!

A whale calf has got a big, gray body and a big tail. It can swim.

calf

This whale calf is swimming in the sea with its mother.

whale

Whale families

A whale calf lives
with its mother.

They do not live
in a group.

The mother is swimming under her calf.

Playing and learning

Baby animals love playing.
They play and they learn!

These lion cubs love playing.

This baby monkey loves running.

This elephant calf loves playing with its trunk.

This whale calf loves playing in the water.

Activities

The key below describes the skills practiced in each activity.

 Spelling and writing

 Reading

 Speaking

 Critical thinking

 Preparation for the Cambridge Young Learners Exams

1 **Circle the correct pictures.**

1 This is a baby monkey.

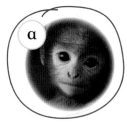

2 This is a group of monkeys.

3 This is a mother and baby whale.

4 This is a group of five elephants.

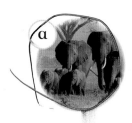

2 Match the words to the pictures.

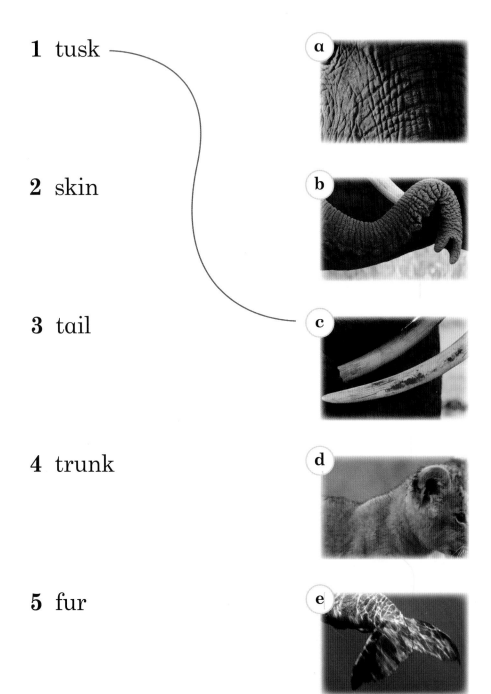

1 tusk

2 skin

3 tail

4 trunk

5 fur

a

b

c

d

e

3 Look and read. Put a ✓ or a ✗ in the boxes. 📖 ✿

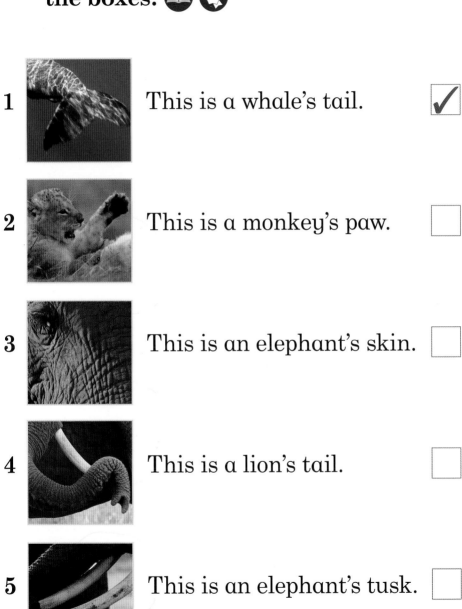

1 This is a whale's tail. ✓

2 This is a monkey's paw. ☐

3 This is an elephant's skin. ☐

4 This is a lion's tail. ☐

5 This is an elephant's tusk. ☐

4 Look and read.
Write *yes* or *no*.

Baby animals

Some baby animals are small.
Some baby animals are big.

Can you see the baby animals?

monkeys

lions

elephants

whales

8   9

1 Some baby animals
are small.   ......yes......

2 Some baby animals
are big.   ....

3 The elephant calves
have got tusks.   ....

4 The baby whale has
got a tail.   ....

5 Work with a friend. Ask and answer *Which?* questions. 🗨️⭐

1

> *Which baby animals are big?*

> *Elephant calves and whale calves are big.*

2 . . . have got tails?

3 . . . live in a group?

4 . . . have got paws?

5 . . . have got gray skin and trunks?

6 Look and read. Write the correct words on the lines. 📖 ✏️ ✻

Monkeys
Baby monkeys are small.

This baby monkey has got brown fur and a pink face.

fur

10

Monkey families
This baby monkey lives with its mother.

They live in a big family group with many monkeys.

12

13

---

fur   group   monkey   monkeys   tails

1 The baby monkey has got brown .... fur ....

2 Monkeys have got long ....

3 This baby .... lives with its mother.

4 They live in a big family ....

5 They live with many ....

7 **Look at the letters.**
Write the words. ✏️ ⭐

Lions
Lion cubs are small.

They have got brown
fur and big paws.

paw

fur

1

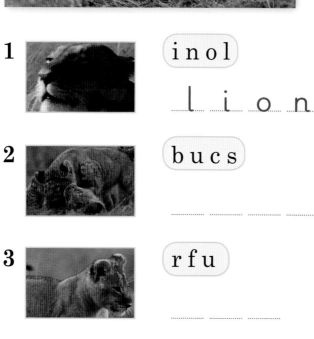

(i n o l)

l i o n

2

(b u c s)

3

(r f u)

4

(w p a)

8 Match the two parts of the sentences. 📖

Elephants

Elephant calves are big.

An elephant calf has got gray skin and a small trunk. It has not got tusks.

calf

elephant

18 This elephant calf is with its mother. 19

1 Elephant calves are

a trunk.

2 An elephant calf has got gray

b tusks.

c big.

3 It has got a small

4 It has not got

d mother.

5 This calf is with its

e skin.

36

9 **Find the words.**

monkey
lion
elephant
whale
group
tail

motmonkeybayielephantbwpgroupefzliontwctailmfwhalewl

10 **Circle the correct sentences.**

Elephant families

An elephant calf lives
with its mother.

They live in a big family
group with many
elephants.

These elephant calves are sleeping
and their mothers are near.

1 a An elephant calf lives
with its father.

b An elephant calf lives
with its mother.

2 a They live in a small family group.

b They live in a big family group.

3 a These elephant mothers
are sleeping.

b These elephant calves
are sleeping.

11 Write *o* or *u*.

1  c‿u‿b

2  li_____n

3  m_____nkey

4  tr_____nk

5  t_____sk

12 **Read the text. Choose the correct words and write them on the lines.**

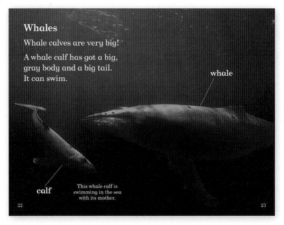

Whales

Whale calves are very big!

A whale calf has got a big, gray body and a big tail. It can swim.

whale

calf

This whale calf is swimming in the sea with its mother.

22   23

---

calves   calf   swim   swimming   tail

Whale [1] _____calves_____ are very big!

This whale [2] _____ has got

a big, gray body. It has got a big

[3] _____, too.

This whale calf can [4] _____

in the sea. It is [5] _____

with its mother.

13 **Write _T_ (true) or _F_ (false).**

1 Whale calves are very small. ....F.......

2 Whale mothers and calves do not live in a family group. ....

3 This whale calf lives in the sea with its mother. ....

4 This whale calf has got a tail. ....

5 This mother whale is swimming above her calf. ....

14 Do the crossword.

¹e	l	e	p	h	a	n	²t

³t

⁴l

Across

1 This big animal has got gray skin.

3 An elephant calf likes playing with this.

4 This mother animal has got cubs.

Down

2 The elephant mother has these, but her calf does not.

3 A whale calf has a big . . .

15 **Look and read. Write *play*, *plays*, or *playing*.**

1 These lion cubs love ⸻ playing ⸻ with their brothers and sisters.

2 They ⸻ with their mother, too.

3 This elephant calf loves ⸻ with its trunk.

4 It ⸻ next to its mother.

16 **Read the questions.**
   Write the answers. 📖 ✏️

1 Which animals love playing?

baby animals

2 Do lion cubs play with their trunks
or paws?
They play with their

3 Do monkeys love running or swimming?
They love

4 Where do whale calves play?
They play in the

17 **Work with a friend. Talk about the two pictures. How are they different? Use the words in the box.** ◯

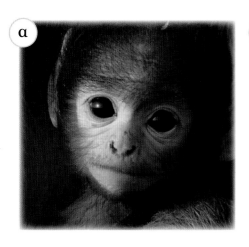

a

b

monkey elephant big calf legs
pink face gray skin trunk arms
brown fur small nose mouth

In picture a, there is a baby monkey.

In picture b, there is a baby elephant.

18 Put the animals in the correct boxes. 📖 ✏️ ❓

monkey   lion   elephant   whale

lives in a group	baby is a calf	has fur
monkey		

19 **Look and read. Put a** ✓ **in the correct boxes.** 📖 ❓

1 Which mother animal is with her small cubs?

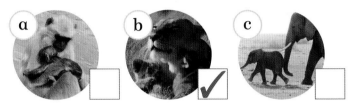

2 Which calf lives in a family group?

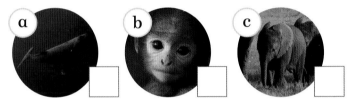

3 Which animal cannot walk or run?

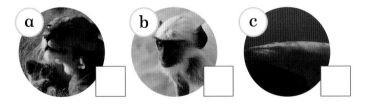

4 Which animal loves running?

Level 1

Anansi Helps a Friend	978-0-241-25409-7
Cinderella	978-0-241-25407-3
The Enormous Turnip	978-0-241-25408-0
On the Farm	978-0-241-25413-4
Cars	978-0-241-28354-7
Jon's Football Team	978-0-241-25411-0
The Magic Porridge Pot	978-0-241-25406-6
In the Garden	978-0-241-26220-7
Fun with Old Things	978-0-241-26219-1
Fairy Friends	978-0-241-28351-6
Peter Rabbit Goes to the Island	978-0-241-25415-8
Topsy and Tim Go to the Zoo	978-0-241-25414-1
Topsy and Tim Go to the Farm	978-0-241-28355-4
The Fair	978-0-241-28357-8
Daddy Pig's Old Chair	978-0-241-28356-1
Rex the Big Dinosaur	978-0-241-29741-4
Peter Rabbit and the Radish Robber	978-0-241-29742-1
Topsy and Tim Go to London	978-0-241-29743-8
On a Boat	978-0-241-29744-5
Baby Animals	978-0-241-29745-2

Now you're ready for Level 2!